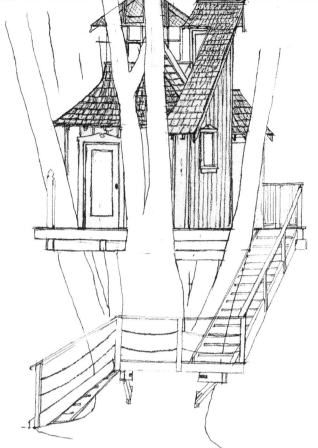

the
treehouse
book

the treehouse book

Peter and Judy Nelson
with David Larkin

Universe Publishing
A David Larkin Book

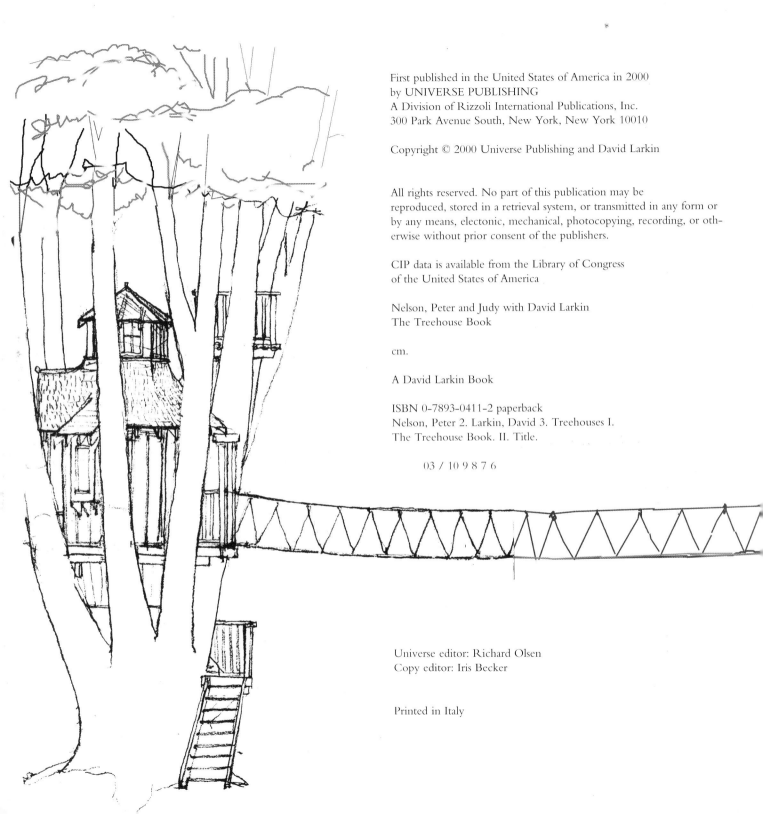

First published in the United States of America in 2000
by UNIVERSE PUBLISHING
A Division of Rizzoli International Publications, Inc.
300 Park Avenue South, New York, New York 10010

CIP data is available from the Library of Congress
of the United States of America

Nelson, Peter and Judy with David Larkin
The Treehouse Book

cm.

A David Larkin Book

ISBN 0-7893-0411-2 paperback
Nelson, Peter 2. Larkin, David 3. Treehouses I.
The Treehouse Book. II. Title.

03 / 10 9 8 7 6

Universe editor: Richard Olsen
Copy editor: Iris Becker

Printed in Italy

Contents

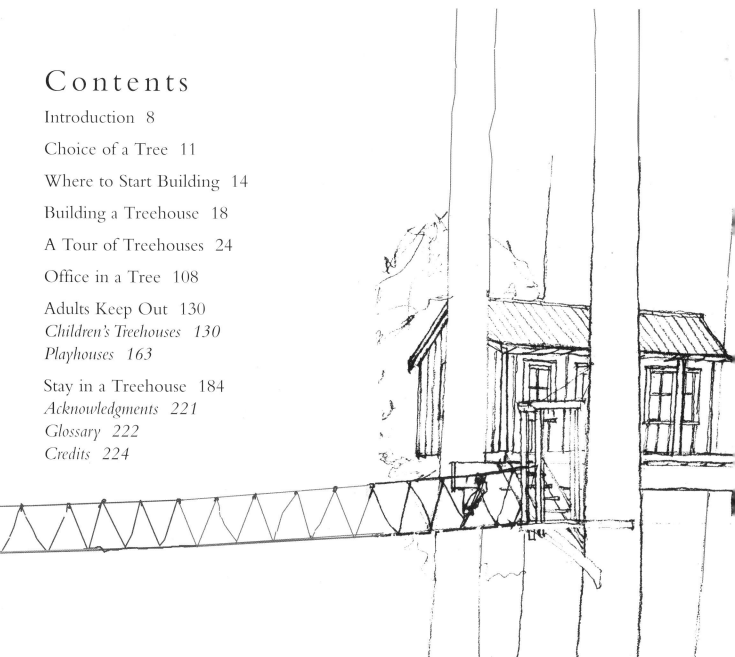

Introduction

IT SEEMS THAT ALMOST EVERYONE LIKES TREEHOUSES, and smiles of recognition turn into grins of enthusiasm as more people discover them and dream about making their own private retreats or family play spaces. And it's nice to remind ourselves that treehouses are built into the oldest and most forgiving, living things on earth.

Anthropologists will attest that treehouse living has been around for a very long time. Even today, in the rain forests of New Guinea, small villages of treehouses are a real escape from the tribal tensions among the clans of the Kombai and Korowai. There is a fear of sorcerers hidden in the edges of the clearings, and a basic need to retreat from areas of heavy flooding. As fears subside, some dwellings come down, from up to 100 feet high on the tops of trees to 10 feet off the ground and resting on stilts. Also, history records treehouses as being built as deliberate follies, as challenges for aboreal designers throughout the ages, for merrymaking, and to keep the spirit of fairy tales alive.

Previous page: a Missouri treehouse erected in a black oak.

The treehouse as a retreat seems to capture the imagination of young and old. The instinct to climb up, then look down to survey a different view of one's locality seems to be fundamental. It's amazing what a distance of a few feet can do to one's perspective of the world. Treehouses represent a return to innocence and an escape from the everyday routine. They can be refreshingly antisocial, deliberately chosen to avoid today's so-called "conveniences." An architect built his retreat deep in the woods because he felt it very important that he had to walk the last quarter of a mile. This was a continual reminder to become careful and selective. He had his own carry-in carry-out campsite. A common feature of retreats is that they are small and hidden away, thus a treehouse can become a place of one's own literally, just because of its small size.

But treehouses can also be social places. We will visit several that were built to entertain, to hang out with friends, or as guest houses. Trees welcome all types. A fine tree by itself attracts one to it as an umbrella. Under the low branches of a single oak you have an outdoor room. Up in a simple treehouse with open doors and windows, filled with dappled light and close to the supporting branches, we can be made aware of the incredible energy that the tree lends itself to make the structure a part of the living tree. As we leave it and look back, we can see it gradually disappear and become just part of the forest.

FAILURE IS ONE OF LIFE'S GREAT TEACHERS. The first Nelson treehouse was in the style of a New England cottage, complete with a porch, shingled roof, and a brick chimney for its fireplace. It was erected in a large cottonwood tree. It came down at two o'clock one morning. The fault in this grand design in miniature was not just those heavy bricks. It was also the wrong

choice of a tree.

Cottonwood is soft and spongy, and only suitable as a shade or windbreak tree. You might think of a treehouse deep in a shady pine wood, but that could mean a lack of light and cool air, with dampness, fungi, and sometimes termites. A deciduous tree has the benefit of open views in the autumn, winter, and spring.

Selecting the right tree is the most important step. For instance, it should not be diseased, rotted, too young, too old, or too small. Maple, oak, fir, and hemlock are among the best species—all strong, stable, and hard. Hickory is durable but extremely tough to drive bolts into. Spruce is susceptible to insects and, because of its shallow roots, a single tree cannot provide effective support, and black walnut has brittle, easy-to-snap branches.

Overleaf are some common and uncommon trees that have held treehouses, along with their heights at maturity and their maximum branch widths.

Left, a treehouse hotel in Kerala, India.

Deciduous Trees

Apple — Its strength, squat shape, and wide branches make it an easy-to-climb favorite for kids' treehouses.
25' high — spread 25'

Apple

Ash — Grows with a straight trunk that is strong enough to bend in high winds. It's a symmetrical tree, with matching or opposite branches that make for a neat treehouse. But look out in the Northeast, where some trees suffer from a blight and a tendency to drop limbs.
Up to 80' high — spread 30'

Ash

Beech — Very slow-growing. The main branches are horizontal to the trunk and the lower ones often point downward. The bark is smooth and often has to withstand many carved initials. Expect visits from squirrels, who love the nuts.
85' high — spread 90'

Beech

Hickory and Pecan — These two are very hard woods that are difficult to bolt to.
90' high — spread 80'

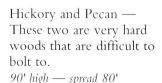

Oak — Nearly all oaks are good hosts to treehouses. Their low-slung branches are easy to climb and are ideal for stoutly built platforms.
Black Oak 100' high — spread 70'
White Oak 85' high — spread 100'
Live Oak 70' high — spread 90'

Oak

Maple — A mature sugar maple tree can yield up to 50 gallons of sugar sap per year, or enough for at least one gallon of syrup. Tapping into the trunk does no harm to the tree. This species is a favorite for Northeast treehouse builders.
85' high — spread 70'
Other suitable maples:
Red 90' high — spread 80'
Black 80' high — spread 40'

Sugar Maple

Sweet Birch — A strong tree with shiny, waterproof bark that used to be stripped off for wintergreen or birch beer. Use in a group.
70' high — spread 50'

Sweet Birch

Sweetgum — The tree itself has the best timber for furnishing the treehouse, being second only to oak as a timber producer. It usually has more open spaces between the branches than an oak tree.
80' high — spread 35'

Conifers, Evergreens, and Tropical Trees

Cypress and Cedar — Although the species are closely related, cedars are usually slimmer and more pinelike than the wider cypress. All are aromatic and resistant to rot. Mature trees have survived forest fires by the thickness of their bark.
150' high — spread 45'

Douglas Fir

Fir — Mature firs are perfect as living posts to support a treehouse, and giants like the Douglas fir can easily support a design that goes around the trunk.
Up to 200' high — spread 50'

Pine — Strong, straight, and fast-growing. Limited amount of support branches. Best to use in a cluster.
Eastern White Pine 140' high — spread 35'
Ponderosa Pine 120' — spread 30'
Sugar Pine 150' — spread 40'

Pine or Hemlock

Hemlock — Use in groups. In most species, before maturity the trunk is hidden from the ground by its evergreen branches. These would have to be trimmed off, sometimes resulting in a rather suburban, ornamental look.
70' high — spread 25'

Redwoods and Sequoias — The world's tallest trees. In previously logged areas, the massive stumps of these endangered trees have sometimes become wonderful hollowed-out playhouses, or platforms for treehouse structures to rest on.
250' high — spread 90'

Sequoia

Banyan — Originally from India, it has made its way to many warm areas. It grows like few other trees, with what are known as adventitious roots. The branches grow downward into the earth to support the tree like pillars supporting a bridge. It grows very quickly outward and downward, and will intertwine with any structure with very interesting results
60' high — spread 100' and wider

Pacific Madrone — A beautiful flowering and fruiting evergreen tree. Very hard wood often with multiple trunks. Keep the kids from snacking on the clusters of edible ripe berries; they'll likely get stomach cramps.
50' high — spread 30'

Palm — Very flexible. Trunk-mount only and through-bolt all connections.
50' high — spread 20'

Trees to Avoid

Cottonwood — Grows quickly to a massive size. Subject to disease. Soft, spongy wood. Keep as a shade tree or a windbreak.
White, Silver, Gray, and *Paper Birches* — Grow quickly but do not live long. A mature tree will reach about 50 feet and then die.
Aspen, or *Poplar* — Grows quickly in abandoned fields in the East, but has a very short lifespan and weak wood.
Poison Sumac — Although its fruit is consumed by birds and animals, it's a very dangerous tree. Its sap causes a skin rash to humans.
Buckeye — The seeds and young leaves are poisonous and the wood is weak.
Western Red Alder — Short-lived with brittle branches.

MANY PEOPLE HAVE FOND MEMORIES OF CAMPING, summers at grandparents farm, and overnight shelters in national parks. These are the impressions that affect the appearance and location of

where to start building

the ideal treehouse. It's often a simpler choice for those with just a few trees and less acreage. Then probably only one tree presents itself as a likely host. If you have the opportunity to choose from a selection of trees and locations, a good way to try out the site is by camping there. Its advantages and problems will soon become evident. An isolated retreat often means carrying or transporting everything having to do with building the treehouse and the means to stay in it.

In less isolated areas, one has to get along with neighbors, and in the suburbs there might be some restrictions. Communities have building codes to ensure safe and healthy structures. They are seen either as being good for all concerned, or as an infringement of individual rights. But codes are here to stay and should be seen as a necessary part of the planning process. It all depends on where you live: some authorities pay strict attention to their zoning laws, and some are lenient about applying those they have.

Local laws vary, but most simple treehouses without plumbing or electricity probably don't need any special building permits or zoning variances. City officials usually don't want to know about them because it can create a public relations nightmare if they come down heavily on a treehouse.

Take the case of Robert Windschauer, of Largo, Florida, who spent months and $5,000 building a treehouse 23 feet up in an old oak tree for his four children and their friends. They loved it but a neighbor complained, arguing that it was a nonpermitted structure too close to his property line. Mr. Windschauer appeared before the local building review board, armed with a petition in favor of "said treehouse" and his four youngsters, ages one to nine, who occupied the front row of the meeting room. The board voted in favor of the Windschauers.

There are times when building inspectors get involved because a neighbor says the treehouse is a eyesore. In Southern California, there are no rules as long as it doesn't exceed the minimum building size of 10-by-10 feet, and 12 feet high, and contains no plumbing. Even building inspectors were kids once. But if they see pipes and electrical cables poking out of the tree and a light on at night, they might rightly assume that someone's living there, and believe that the structure should conform to the local code. It's when someone tries to outsmart them that a structure can be disapproved.

A treehouse is squeezed into the city.

You should know or find out which zoning laws (like setback requirements) apply if you think there might be problems and, if in doubt, pay a visit to the local building officer to save trouble. Tact and diplomacy might be required if you are aware of possible restrictions. In many cases, building officials might be hearing for the first time about somebody planning to erect a treehouse. The word "treehouse" may not appear in their code book, and they could be intrigued and helpful.

One day we got a call from a Jonathan Fairoaks, who had seen our first book and liked it, but said we had to meet so he could describe how Peter Nelson was "killing trees with kindness." Jonathan, a member of The International Society of Arborculture, is a certified arborist. Also, he lives in a treehouse. He arrived in Fall City and we went aloft into the trees above our treehouse, where he pointed out what we were doing wrong. Since then we have become friends and work together on the best ways to support treehouses and keep the trees happy.

Here is Jonathan Fairoaks on
Finding and Preserving a Tree for Your Treehouse

Is this tree all right for me? Look closely, does the branch structure look hospitable for a treehouse? Building closer to the ground allows for more possiblities in terms of strength, center of gravity, and construction of additional levels. Look at how the branches are attached. If the union is *V*-shaped, it is not as strong as a *U*-shape. You can use a *V*-shape, but you should support the branch juncture with a cable. Are there twists, turns, fractures, and hollow spaces, cankers or wounds on the trunk and branches?

Do not be dismayed if your tree appears to have problems. Often, it is possible to design the treehouse to strengthen the weak portions. A certified arborist can assist by pruning, crown-thinning, and cabling. If you are going to invest your time and money into this arboreal creation, set aside a portion of your investment for having the tree inspected and cared for. For as little as $100, an arborist can substantially strengthen a problem that may cause disaster if left unattended. Many arborists will visit free of charge. I strongly recommend making sure the foundation of the tree is in good shape. The tree in the forest shows the top of its root flares. Sometimes around homes the soil has been built up over the roots. This soil should be removed and the roots should be inspected

Jonathan says that almost any tree can support a treehouse or a part of one:

Peter and I have designed a suspension method of mounting treehouses, which is described in Peter's Home Tree Home *(pp 51–56). You will be able to use limbs and trees above your proposed foundation height, allowing much more flexibility in design. We are currently building a treehouse in which one entire 16x18-foot section is being supported by a cable from a branch 22 feet overhead. This branch is in turn supported by two cables going to branches on the opposing side of the tree, thereby adding stability to the other side of the tree as well as supporting the supporting branch. A fourth cable connects the other two branches creating a triangle. The triangle of cable is used universally by arborists to add strength and stability to large trees with spreading crowns (see figure 1). This "new" technology makes it possible to use a tree which otherwise may be considered by some to branch out too frar from the ground. This same idea can be applied to long spans—16 feet and more— between trees (see figure 2). Remember to install eyebolts perpendicular to the load force so that you rely on the sheer strength of the bolt, not the thread-holding ability.*

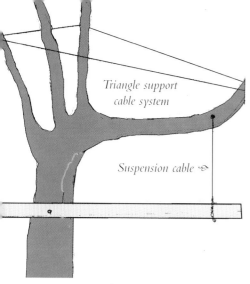

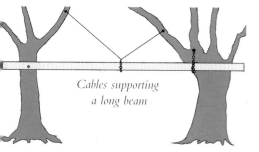

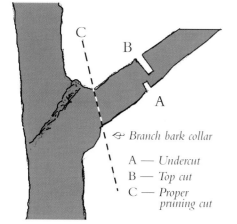

FIGURE 1

*Triangle support
cable system*

Suspension cable ✎

FIGURE 2

*Cables supporting
a long beam*

FIGURE 3

✎ *Branch bark collar*

A — *Undercut*
B — *Top cut*
C — *Proper
      pruning cut*

for girdling (roots that grow over primary roots, thus strangling them), rotting bark, and any other sign of poor health.

The ideal tree will be in good health, about 144 feet tall, with the main scaffold branches beginning to radiate out horizontally at about 20 to 40 feet from the ground. This character will be well balanced with branches spread about four to 12 feet from one another around the trunk. Their points of attachment will be *U*-shaped. The growth of smaller branches will be even throughout the canopy. The root flares will be prominent and exposed from about three to five feet from the trunk of the tree. The entire area under the drip line will be provided with essential elements, compost, and a mycorhizae cocktail—available at good garden centers—and covered over with three to five inches of composted wood chips made from branches of the same type of tree.

Its habitat will be near a stream or body of water from which its roots will derive the liquid sustenance necessary for life. If this is not the case, it will be in an area that collects rainwater without being flooded by it. Otherwise an irrigation system should be provided to supply a copious quantity of water, bimonthly, away from the trunk to an area 15 to 20 feet beyond the dripline. Remember that the area beneath the treehouse will not receive rainwater.

If you find the need to remove branches, try to take only the dead, damaged, and diseased ones. When the treehouse is up in the crown of the tree, you may need to lighten it to compensate for the extra weight and windsail effect. Take no more than one-third of the branches, preferably from the top and outside of the crown. Be certain to make pruning cuts as close as possible to the branch bark collar. If large branches are being removed, remember to make a small undercut about six inches away from the collar. Drop the branch from the top of the cut, then make the final cut next to the collar (see figure 3). If the collar is not apparent to you, try to keep your cuts as small as possible.

Do not leave stubs, cut into a branch bark collar, top trees, use climbing spikes, paint wounds, fill in cavities, grow grass, or allow vehicles underneath.

Do respect your aboreal friend, and then you will have a companion for life.

This treehouse is 60 feet off the ground.

IMAGINE A SIMPLE PLATFORM UP IN THE TREE REACHED by an apple picker's ladder. Above the platform is a hammock strung between strong branches, and strung above that is an awning to stop raindrops or caterpillars from falling on your tired brow. From there you might want to consider something a little more sheltering.

The idea of actually building a treehouse has not been in the minds of most adults since the age of 12, but for those who want to turn those daydreams into structures, here are some basic points we use in

building a treehouse

along with valuable experience that we and other treehouse builders have gained along the way.

All treetop habitats attest to the passion and determination behind these treehouse urges. The construction of such branch-top creations ranges from expensive to low-cost. There is a treehouse in Florida, for example, that cost more than $200,000. An equally beautiful treehouse on Camano Island in Washington was built almost exclusively from salvaged and recycled materials, and cost only the time to put it together (which was considerable). Tree-dwellers agree, however, that living and spending time in a tree is a full-body, mind-centering, and spiritually cleansing experience. All you really need to be careful of is the building inspector.

The typical treehouse platform consists of beams, floor joists, and floorboards. The size of the lumber will depend on the dimension of your house. It's important not to stress the beams or the floors joists.

Recently we received a call from a Chicago man who was building his treehouse. He said he was using a two-by-four that was spanning 16 feet and wanted to know if that was enough support. We told him to take it down immediately.

We recommend consulting a basic spanning chart, available at building supply stores. If your beams are 10 feet apart, for example, the chart might tell you to use 2-by-10 joists spaced 16 inches apart.

We built a treehouse in Japan. One of the rules was that the bark of the trees should not be pierced with nails, screws, or bolts. We thought that following this Buddhist way was worth trying. The tree was protected by thick rubber rings and the platform was clamped by bolts. Sadly, it didn't work: the treehouse is slowly slipping toward the ground.

We are partial to the one-tree variety, where the platform rests in an open hand of limbs or on a series of bracket supports encircling a tall, straight trunk. The best house for a novice, however, is the four-tree: secure two stout beams to four well-spaced trees, and you've got a frame on which to build your platform.

If you choose sturdy, mature trees and build relatively close to the ground, chances are you can get by with a fixed platform—one that is anchored directly to the trees with bolts—rather than a free-floating design. As a rule of thumb, keep the platform in the bottom eighth of the tree. For instance, if your tree is 80 feet tall, the platform should be no higher than 10 feet.

More than anything else—except, perhaps, the proximity to the ground—the platform, your only point of contact with the tree, is what defines a treehouse. A strong platform is crucial both to your treehouse and to the well-being of those who will frequent it. It's where you'll meet your toughest design challenges, such as how to accommodate growth and motion.

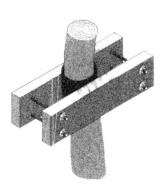

Building Points

Choose your trees carefully. Maple, oak, fir, and hemlock are good, but black walnut is notoriously brittle, and ash trees have a propensity to shed branches.

The shape of a treehouse should be dictated by the tree rather than the builder.

Allow ample time. If building something on the ground might take twice as long as you anticipate, figure three or four times your expectations for a treehouse.

Build as much as you can on the ground, then assemble it in the tree.

Trees bend and the treehouses must bend with them.

Wear a hardhat and use a harness and a safety line when working up in a tree.

Treehouses are not meant to be permanent structures.

Although a treehouse may last for years, a tree will last longer. Trees live longer than humans, but they do die.

Stability

Should you be nervous about the stability of your platform, don't take it out on the tree by driving a dozen nails into the branch. Instead, make your bolts count. Use three-quarter-inch (or bigger) galvanized lag bolts. And never space them less than a foot apart. Michael Garnier produces a 1 1/4" treehouse bolt (the Garnier Limb) that has been tested to withstand 6,000 pounds. Unfortunately, most people who build treehouses don't understand trees. Our friend the arborist Jonathan Fairoaks points out that because of the way a tree heals itself—by clotting wounds with sap—it might treat two close punctures as one, causing everything in between them to rot. Another caution is to allow branches or the trunk to expand outward in circumference as the tree develops. Judicious pruning may also be needed to lighten the tree's load to compensate for the burden of the treehouse. In this case, if you have any doubts, it would be prudent to get the help of a qualified arborist rather than a tree surgeon.

A big treehouse in a small tree, or at the top of a large tree, will catch a lot of wind and might, in extreme conditions, act as a sail and cause the tree or branches to be blown down. It probably wouldn't come to this, but the forces exerted on the treehouse will be larger, so strong anchorage is required. You should attach to the trunk and choose areas with thicker branches if building higher.

If you build in a single tree, the points where you fix supports will need to be strong enough to hold the weight of the part of the treehouse they're supporting. It's simpler to build with a few long supporting beams than lots of smaller ones. This still means several attachment points; e.g., four branches in one tree. For a one-story treehouse, a minimum branch thickness for four attachment points is about six inches. If you have more than one story or the extra weight of overhanging sections, then you may need 10 inches or more. If your branches don't allow for this, use more attachment points so that the weight is efficiently spread out. If you are planning to use two or more trunks or trees, you must be careful when fitting supports. As the trees continue to grow outward and upwards, the joints between the tree-house and tree will be subject to stress from the weight and movement of people inside, and winds, all of which can cause twisting. In a strong wind, the trees will sway and twist. You should not try to restrict the movement because doing so could destroy your house.

Once the platform is in place, you can begin constructing the rest of the house. Maybe you want a simple box with a trapdoor and a roof that slopes from front to back. Our most important advice for this stage is to build as much of the house as possible on the ground. Up in the tree, space and gravity will be working against you and you will have to keep descending to the ground for building materials and your heavier tools. Also, employing a block and tackle to hoist finished sections of walls and the roof will save you from having to hang off the outside of the house to paint or to tack shingles. Be sure to anchor your block and tackle to the trunk of the tree. A single pulley works well for hauling up crates of light tools and other small items. Often that pulley remains in place as a momento of the construction. It's a reminder of how useful it was, and remains the best way to lift a cooler into the tree.

The best-shaped tree is one that opens like a hand at a reasonable distance from the ground.

Any load-bearing branch should be at least six inches in diameter.

A treehouse for adults can be any height, but one for kids shouldn't be much higher than eight feet.

Don't cut the bark and the cambium layer any more than you absolutely have to; cutting more than halfway around will kill the tree or branches.

Consider your means of access. You can pull a rope ladder up after you, but it's hard to climb. A rigid ladder is easier, but not as portable. Purists may blanch, but the best approach might just be conventional steps.

Make rails strong. People lean on them as they look out. The minimum height for railings under the Uniform Building Code is 36 inches high.

Keep everyone from walking under the tree during construction —especially children.

Use eyebolts that pass all the way through branches or bolt into the trunk rather than pass cables over the bark.

21

Building Points

Make sure that you use high quality wood for main support beams and posts.

Slant your roof. Otherwise, leaves or snow will pile up and add weight to your treehouse.

Use one-inch threaded bars or large bolts instead of nails for strong attachment.

During construction, set up a pulley to lift wood easily, and avoid throwing a line over a branch. Tie ropes or telephone cords to hammers and electric drills so that when you drop them (and you will) they don't fall all the way down to the ground.

Use galvanized fittings to avoid rust and possible structural failure.

Use screws instead of nails for connecting wall panels and framework that sometimes get twisted or otherwise stressed during use.

If you have to hammer a nail near the end of a piece of wood, it may split the wood. If you don't have a drill handy to make the pilot holes, take the nail and place it on a hard surface with the point up. Hammer the point so the nail is blunt. It will now cut through the fibers, rather than forcing them apart, and the wood won't split.

Connections

We have seen some good advice on the Internet for first-time treehouse builders. Patrick Fulton's website in particular gives accounts of his own experience that confirms our own, especially in regard to getting the right connections.

A nail hammered into a tree will not damage it. A nail simply pierces a small hole through the bark and into the dead structural wood within. If you have a branch with a diameter of 10 inches or so, the nail affected area amounts to under 1 percent, which is harmless.

Admittedly, if you hammer hundreds of nails all around the trunk, it probably will damage it. More damage is caused by loose supporting beams than nails. If the wood is allowed movement, it will rub against the tree, exposing living tissues and eventually wearing patches of it away. However, a healthy tree should be able to survive even this—similar to a branch being removed.

A bolted supporting beam for a California treehouse is backed up by a safety cable.

Galvanized nails are a lot better than standard steel because they do not rust. Rusting causes brown staining of wood, will weaken the nail, and might suddenly snap when you put a load on it. Galvanized nails do not harm trees—the galvanizing material (zinc) stops the nails from rusting because it is nonreactive in wet conditions. There may be a problem if the wood is slightly acidic, like oak, because this can corrode the nail. However, it is still a much slower process than rusting steel.

We recommend bolts because they are easier to fit than huge nails, and a lot stronger. A properly sized bolt won't bend under weight as some nails have done, and one bolt is equivalent to several nails, thus causing less damage to the tree. It's also very difficult to remove large nails from trees. Bolts are better if you have to take your treehouse down—the drilled hole will seal itself up again.

You need eyebolts for any cables. Trees have all their living parts in the first two inches or so in from the bark (mostly just under the bark), so drilling a hole right through the tree will not damage it any more than a nail would. You would normally have to cut away the bark nearly half the way around before a tree will start to suffer. This is why pinching by cables kills—it strangles the tree by cutting off the food supply. Similarly, don't put cables around branches for the same reason.

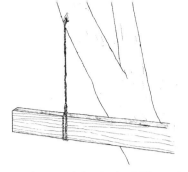

A suspended-point load. The most flexible of treehouse supports.

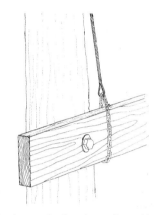

A fixed-point load with a safety cable. Good for treehouses close to the ground.

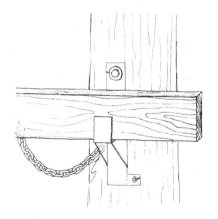

A floating-point load. Good when using more than one tree. The Garnier Limb would be an excellent alternative to this custom made bracket.

A Tour of Treehouses

Our company, Treehouse Workshop, designed and built this treehouse for the parents of an old friend. The location, in a magnificent group of redwoods, overlooks a beautiful creek. The owners love having an evening glass of wine on the curved deck.

This getaway is hidden on the edge of family vineyards. These scenes show the treehouse before occupation. The shingle-finished building is in continuous use by all generations of the family, and there's a loft for extra sleeping accommodations. The interior is lined throughout with paneling, and the old farmhouse doors were used.

This picture is taken from a distance to show the beauty of the setting.
It shows an antique arched window, a large bay window, and a back deck that measures 6-by-9 feet.

Located in the Santa Cruz mountains, this 300-square-foot treehouse, designed by Thomas Kern, is built 40 feet up, around the trunk of a huge redwood. It's poised above a sparkling creek and looks out in all directions into a magical forest. Access to the building is a 38-foot-long cable suspension bridge that's a mere 10 yards behind the main house. The treehouse itself is made of redwood and merges beautifully with its host tree and surroundings.

This view is taken from the ground 40 feet away, during construction.

Looking at the front of the house from the side of the bridge.
The interior is set up as a working office, with the power cables
buried underground following the direction of the bridge.

Standing on the bridge landing looking at the front door of the treehouse.
The bridge is great fun to walk across.

With a husband, four daughters, and assorted pets, the last thing a Seattle woman wanted was the added responsibility of maintaining a big vacation home. But her family really wanted some kind of getaway on their 10-acre undeveloped property, on Washington island, about 40 minutes from their home. So she compromised and, for about $25,000, we built them a treehouse.

The unfurnished interior.

Nestled in the midst of four pine trees, the two-story, 14-by-14-foot structure is about 10 feet off the ground. It has two porches and can sleep seven people in sleeping bags and futons. It doesn't have electricity, so when the family spends the night up there—which happens about once a month—they use candles and bring up an ice chest full of food and drink.

After restoration.

The original treehouse, looking newer than the rebuilt version.

The balusters on the rebuilt porch are made from hemlock branches lopped from surrounding trees.

Several months after it was finished, we received a call from the owners. Arriving at their getaway, they found that a huge storm had wrecked a good part of it. They were very nice about it, considering the state of their discovery. And, very importantly, it was not all the fault of the storm. What looked like a perfectly good salvaged log used as a sructural support was weak, which led to the collapse when the four supporting trees were under stress. We learned a lesson: to be really careful about where to use recycled materials. The treehouse was resurrected, and you can see in the pictures the old and the new treehouse, with the new one looking older than the original.

The restored treehouse.

Morningwood Treehouse

There is sometimes a chromosonal impulse to build a treehouse—a guy thing. Built by two friends as an escape from their respective houses, this is a maple treehouse for 40-year-old boys who actually spend more time admiring it from the ground than in it. When they do make the climb it's to watch sports on a portable TV, which is powered by car batteries. On occasion, they are known to spend the night if a game goes into overtime.

Because the soil of the surroundings is so rich, owner Ed McBee has developed a lush garden with paths stemming out from the base of the maple tree. He often spends time hanging out, reading, and relaxing on the midlevel deck, and he can climb onto the treehouse roof, which is used to tee-off golf balls.

The structure at the end of this climb toward the sky features a large deck with French doors that face the jagged silhouette of the Cascades. Also included are two neatly designed foldout bunks, a desk, and the world's simplest plumbing system. "It takes us four seconds to hit the ground," says McBee's buddy, Randy Geiger.

The sign posted on the tree isn't very intimidating, but the climb is. It's up the ladder, through a hole leading to a deck, then up another trunk via alpine petons leading to a trapdoor. On the top deck, there's a view of the Cascades.

Treesnakes

The best of both worlds is to have a secluded treehouse on its own riverbank. A couple who like to call themseves Hazel and Filbert have built one on their 15 acres of north central Minnesota woodland. They had camped on their original 10 acres for over 10 years, but it wasn't until 1996, when they acquired five additional acres, that they got serious about building a treehouse there. Hazel and Filbert take the stewardship of their land around Treesnakes seriously.

They care for the environment through forest replantation and wildlife-habitat protection, and enjoy kayaking the river rapids and fly-fishing. Three years ago, they had the notion of putting a treehouse along the river's edge. Hazel found our book *Treehouses,* and after "scouting" trees up and down the river, they found a beautiful clump of red maples growing in the river bottom. After careful review of the book, they started the construction process.

Hazel continues the story: *Since we didn't even have a trail into the property, that became our first year's task. Eventually, we cleared the trail and the hauling phase began in earnest. Every lick of material was carried, hauled, carted, or wrestled down the trail by my husband. We obviously weren't in a hurry and our motto was always "Keep it simple." With the need to accommodate two dogs, the "bridge" from the top of the bank to the treehouse solved this problem. The front of the treehouse is anchored by the large pin oak out front and a small footing on the left edge. The next phase will be finishing the observation deck that is out over the east canopy of maples, behind the treehouse structure. This deck is approximately 25 feet above the floodplain. After so many years of trail hauling, how nice it will be! It was a little difficult to decide to actually hire the road builder this summer—something was definitely lost, but much has been gained as well. The roadwork was finished this fall. Now we can actually begin building another treehouse on the new five acres and start the long-term construction of an earthbound cabin.*

The main part of the house is built on seven Douglas firs.

The Scurlock Treehouse

In 1997 the trilevel treehouse in Olympia, Washington, built by notorious bank robber William Scott Scurlock, was put up for sale along with the rest of his wooded acres. "The estate had debts that we couldn't pay unless we sold the property," said retired minister Bill Scurlock, who, with wife Mary Jane, is executor of his son's estate.

The son called "Scotty" robbed more than 15 banks in the Northwest before the Thanksgiving 1996 pursuit —often wearing white makeup and theatrical disguises, and wielding a gun. Following a $1 million heist at a Lake City bank, Scurlock was tracked to a camper in a North Ravenna backyard, where he met his end. When FBI agents checked out his property, they seized semiautomatic weapons, makeup, fake mustaches, and more than $20,000 in cash in the barn and treehouse.

View of the main stairway. Originally, access to the treehouse was by rope ladder with a firehouse pole for a quick—and fun—exit. This was later removed for safety reasons.

The sundeck. To the left (not shown) is the bathroom. There are only two walls—just enough to insure privacy—so the user can enjoy the view while showering or using the toilet.

Scurlock was described by friends as a daredevil, dreamer, poet, and avid mountain climber who was happiest when he had a hammer in his hand. The roughly 1,500-square-foot treehouse, where he lived on and off for more than a decade, was his pet project. Construction of the angled treehouse, with 30 windows and sited high in the boughs of a stand of second-growth firs and cedars, began in 1980 at 30 feet; this one-man job kept going up level after level. It included plumbing, wiring, a wood-stove, a firehouse pole for quick descent, large picture windows, and a sundeck with a shower at 75 feet. He called the deck "an angel's landing pad."

A poem, read at Scurlock's memorial service, began:

> *To be in a treehouse*
> *is to be inside and yet outside,*
> *to be free and yet protected,*
> *to be held in the air and yet rooted,*
> *held*

The kitchen features an electric stove.

Woodstove area. This stove heats the entire treehouse.
The wood is hauled up from the ground through a trapdoor in the floor.

Second-floor sitting area. The ladder on the right leads to the sleeping loft.

John Schultz's Treehouse

When we received this picture from John Schultz, of Springfield, Illinois, it accompanied a letter about building the treehouse. We thought the story of his progress, experimentation, problems, and success was very well described. Here, we are glad to reprint it almost entirely.

I bought your book, *Home Tree Home*, and ended up building what you see in the pictures. It sits a maximum of 22 feet off the ground at the peak of the roof. It's a 6-by-10-foot house with a 3-by-8-foot front porch. I had four pages of wall/roof sketches so I could estimate the materials required, but I basically figured the rest as I went along.

The house still requires a coat of paint on the pre-primered hardboard siding, some caulking, and stain/preservative on the trim and front porch. I'll save that work until the warm weather comes. It has a 40-degree pitch on the roof, which, by the way, is a complete mistake. I sketched the roof to have a 4/10 pitch.

Unfortunately, my brain equated "40" degrees with "4/10," so I cut my two-by-fours at 40 degrees to make my roof trusses. A 4/10 pitch is actually around 22 degrees. Anyway, the mistake was both good and bad. The goofy thing is that an adult can comfortably stand inside the tree-house, as the ceiling is over six feet tall at the cross brace on the truss. The house is 10 feet tall at the peak of the roof, even though I only built four-foot walls. The bad thing is that the shingling process was downright dangerous. The treehouse is built on a rather steep-sloped ravine, and we had a hell of a time getting my 22-foot extension ladder tied off and stable enough to work from the deep side at the back of the treehouse.

In addition, all the shingling was done in 30- to 35-degree weather. I split my thumb with a hammer on the second-to-last roofing nail on the whole roof. My thumb hurt less than the other four fingers, which were thawing from frostbite. Once the roof was done, I was glad I made the mistake on the pitch. Here's a few other design features:

★ The triangular base is composed of treated 2x6s attached to three oak trees using 10-inch-long, 1/2" lag screws. Those six attachments are the only damages to the trees, including the roots. I used two-inch plumbing nipples as spacers to allow for trunk growth. I slotted the 2x6s to allow the board to give a little if the trunks swayed in the wind.

★ I used 1/8" acrylic to make the windows. I fabricated the door and windows out of 2x2s ripped lengthwise. All windows and doors open inward and close with hinges on the side. The exterior trim hides the edges well and makes for a clean look. Each of the five windows has a ledge made from scrap deck board.

★ I have a trapdoor in the floor of the house. I used a piano hinge in the floor to swing a 22-by-27-inch door.

★ The trim (1x3 batten boards) and fascia (1x6) are cedar.

★ I originally planned to rely on the three oak trees I used as the sole means of support for the treehouse. However, I "cheated" by sinking three 4x4 posts at midspan of each side of the triangle. Now, only the square-footage limits the weight you can put in that treehouse. It's solid.

The treehouse took two people approximately 60 hours to complete. The material cost around $1,200, but at least $300 of that was due to my inexperience (just one example is that the hinges I originally purchased for the five windows were way too big, so I had to buy smaller ones) and the lack of a contractor's discount.

The inside of the treehouse has no finish work. That's up to my young son and his imagination. It also has no electrical, plumbing, or insulation, though I could install these things if I wanted. It is, however, watertight and sturdy.

I'm proud of this project because it's almost perfectly level and square, despite the fact that the only big wood projects I've ever done were a doghouse/kennel and a 12-by-18-foot back deck. It's a unique building, and it seems to capture the imagination of anybody else that sees it for the first time.

Thanks for providing the inspiration and practical knowledge necessary for me to convince myself I could do this.

We have mentioned before that the ideal host for a treehouse is a tree that opens up like the fingers on an upturned palm. Normally a Douglas fir doesn't resemble such an ideal tree, but at one time in its 300-year history, this tree had its top sheared off in a storm. It recovered by sending its massive boughs upward like fingers, with two main trunks reaching 150 feet high. Nestling in this arrangement is a large, nearly complete treehouse. Its owner-builder carries on finishing it as a one-man job, but he needed the help of two others to erect the 35-foot-high platform.

Although large, the treehouse is hard to see because of thick foliage from the additional branches.

The builder admires the work of the early 20th-century Arts and Crafts architects Greene and Greene. Through the fir needles you can see the deep overhanging eaves and exposed purlins that compliment their style.

Below the straight stairway there's a connection of wonderfully arranged steps assembled from gathered driftwood.

Except for the kitchen area with its fitted stove and refrigerator, the interior is not finished,
although it's ready to be lived in. The angles and fittings follow
a simplified Greene and Greene look—leaded windows, heavy beams, and
built-in, rather than movable, furniture.

This treehouse is built in a California valley oak that is estimated to be between 70 and 100 years old. The host tree recently withstood the onslaught from severe El Niño storms. Fifty yards away from the treehouse, a 40-foot cypress and a giant ash were wrecked by gusts up to 75 miles per hour. Our owner-builder friend Mark reported that he stood under the tree during the peak of the storm and it rode it out beautifully.

Mark's young son and his friends and cousins use the treehouse continually. So, after the storms, Mark added five lodgepole pine posts underneath for added protection. He has also been asked on two occasions if he is interested in putting up more treehouses. His style is obviously popular in Southern California.

A unique feature is the spiral staircase designed and built by Mark and a friend. Although the rail came ready-made, the treads are wider than on conventional iron spirals, and are much easier to use. The wooden treads are covered with a weatherproof, nonslip treatment that dries into the wood.

A lot of attention was spent finishing the green tin roof where the tree comes through in four places. Fitting the flashing around the branch exits was a tricky operation.

Branches also exit through the walls.

Mark followed some of our design suggestions and says that the pine construction and interior finish contrasts perfectly with the the natural bark colors of the oak.

A Ponderosa Treehouse

Albert Green got the treehouse bug at the raising of Saltspring treehouse, in British Columbia, and three years later we visited him and built a treehouse on his ranch in Pleasant Valley, Montana. The previous year Albert selected the spot, on a small knoll 250 yards from his house. It was a small stand of ponderosa pines—one tall and arrow-straight, 180 feet tall and 14 feet around the base, with two younger ones that might be used for additional support if necessary. It turned out that the single pine was enough to support the treehouse, and the smaller, slimmer pair now just create a little more shade and seclusion. A perfect spot. We noticed, too, that the main branches began about 40 feet up, so the treehouse could be high, and so it came to be.

We have remarked before about having a little ceremony before starting work. We hold one for each treehouse we build. Placing one's hand on the tree and asking it for permission comes easy. An explanation of intention and a promise to treat the tree with respect bodes well for the relationship between the tree and those who will build in it. After these brief words, we bury a clove of garlic at the base of the trunk as a symbol to ward off disease and evil spirits.

A treehouse builder's props on the first day: block and tackle, climbing ropes with a tensile strength of over 5,000 pounds, and a milk crate to carry the tools. The first bracket is in place—firmly held by 10x3/4-inch lag bolts.

Right: Three of the eight supporting braces and their beams, which will fan out from the trunk. The braces are set and bolted into customized brackets.

The first wall is carefully lifted up to the finished deck.

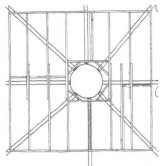

The deck framework.

The tree could easily support an umbrella-style foundation just as the one at Saltspring (see page 95). The straight trunk was just right for allowing the level beams to fan out just like the ribs of a parasol. With the trunk dead-center, our design surrounds it: a square deck around the small circle as the tree comes up through the house.

The floor plan.

The last wall goes up.

The treehouse is designed as two boxes that meet at right angles. The living room is 7-by-11-feet and the bedroom is 6-by-7-feet.

66

Albert's treehouse has galvanized-metal roofing, which is light, efficient, and easy to install. Rain falling on a metal roof is a wonderful sound.

As a personal touch, we like to use railing posts fashioned from the same species of tree. The tops of the rails should always be at least three feet off the deck.

Above right

The built-in window seat rests on a floor that has two-inch-thick rigid foam insulation to ward off the chill on Montana summer nights.

There just wasn't time to build a ladder when the treehouse was finished, so we continued to use the removable extension ladder used in construction. On reflection we decided that it should become the regular means of access, because the treehouse was visible from a road; a retractable ladder would make the treehouse unreachable in Albert's absence.

This is one of a pair treehouses that float between a canopy of ohia trees and a forest of hachu tree ferns on the slopes of Mount Hualalai in Hawaii. Both houses are built in the Hawaiian cottage style with wraparound decks. They are among the best-appointed treehouses we have seen, with iron clawfoot bathtubs, high-rank toilets, hot and cold running water, centrally plumbed gas lanterns, and queen-sized bunk beds.

Amid a forest of maple, pine, and hemlock, Brother Francis reads on the steps of a one-man treehouse. He helped to build it in a Franciscan retreat that serves as a hermitage in western Massachussetts.

Right by it, perched on a rock, is another tiny structure, which is a one-man chapel.

During contsruction.

John Kirchmier said he had such a good time helping a local professional contractor friend he engaged to build his treehouse, that he sent us these pictures. The treehouse has a view of the Atlantic Ocean, as well as a view of Albemarle Sound. It has a tin roof and a complete walk-around deck. It is 20 feet up on one side and overlooks a little valley on the other side.

74

The Whiting treehouse, in eastern New York, rests on a twin-forked, middle-aged oak tree, with one trunk going through the building. The structure seems to cantilever out widely on one side, but in fact the design was carefully worked out; two firmly embedded steel tubes give the required extra support. The tubes were erected by the engineer builder and his son as part of the specially designed elevator, which is the only way to travel up and down. The driving motor that raises and lowers the one-at-a-time passenger car is cleverly hidden in the roof of the "shaft."

Above is the treehouse platform and the elevator roof, which holds the electric motor. As you reach the deck, you exit the car by simply raising the two joined bars out of their grooves. As you descend, you replace them just before pushing the button.

The builders' next plan is to use the elevator supports as pipes for the treehouse's water supply, with connections running under the deck.

A woman asked Matt Peters, a young builder, to realize a dream of the treehouse she never had as a child. Nothing complicated, perhaps just a platform up between the oaks. As Matt got to work, her husband asked if he could help, and the structure began to grow in scope and detail. Each time she appeared on the scene, the three of them worked on completing the dream. Today the treehouse is well finished throughout. The interior fittings are oak and the floor is hardwood.

On each side of the front door, there are angled windows that open inward so they don't intrude on the deck. The gable end of the roof overhangs the deck so the pulley at the top, kept in place from the time of construction, can lift things right to the front door.

Mike Caveney's wife Tina plays her harp 18 feet up on the deck of their well-equipped and partly solar-powered Pasadena willow treehouse. Apart from her music, which adds to the ambience, Mike says it's also a great place to watch the Rose Bowl game on TV and hear the real crowd cheering nearby.

The evocative setting was used in a test shot for the cover of Tina Caveney's CD *Branching Out*.

The main deck with stairs to the overnight treehouse.

The complex of treehouses from a distance. The small building on the ground houses the generator and water heater.

Joy Bennett has a very interesting compound of treehouses, all connected and on different levels. One deck supports a sauna and a second is for cooking, while the others are for relaxing and sleeping.

A view of the lower deck and the sauna.

The Carringtons built a weekend treehouse on several acres they have in the Texas countryside. It's spread in some oak trees, shingled, and has a tin roof. They liked it so much that Dale Carrington put down his *Tarzan* book and built a simpler backyard version at their home in Houston for weekday use. It is a peaceful place in the midst of the city to enjoy their morning coffee and papers, and they have plans to screen it in to enjoy the cool evening breezes.

On the side of a hill above San Carlos, California, David DeBella built this treehouse in one of the many pines in the area. This tree, a rare Monterey pine, had a divided trunk. It is a good example of letting the shape of the tree dictate the design of the treehouse. The deck rests in the area where the trunk divides, and the treehouse takes advantage of the opening space at a different angle.

The platform is 18 feet off the ground. The treehouse matches the shape and exterior colors of the bigger main house, just 35 feet away. Although tall enough to be used by adults, the short distance from the house and the power connections enable David's children to play safely and watch their own TV programs.

Perched high above a Eureka neighborhood in a split-trunked redwood is one of
two treehouses erected by a fisherman. It is now owned by a couple who let
children play there when they are closely supervised.

With our friend Nat Ross, we built an unusual treehouse in an unusual tree for
Doug Thron, the environmentalist and nature photographer. The Thron treehouse is built
as a good example of a suspended-load foundation. The suspension method is very flexible;
the structure hangs from high-strength cables that are held by eye-lags screwed into the
branches above. The treehouse rests in an ancient madrone tree (see page 13) that has five
separate trunks, each an average of two feet in diameter at the base.

Aloft in the madrone tree, Jonathan Fairoaks lops judiciously.

After some guidance from our friend the arborist Jonathan Fairoaks, we created
a 15-by-16-foot, solar-powered model, complete with sleeping loft, about 20 feet off
the ground in this majestic madrone tree 30 miles east of Willow Creek, California.
It provides unusual accommodations for some overnighters as part of Doug's California
Ancient Forest Adventures—backpacking trips through old-growth redwood forests
amid spectacular alpine settings.

Paul Brozen says that if a tree can grow in Brooklyn, then a treehouse can be built in Queens. Completed in three months, the treehouse has seen lots of use by his young sons Brendan and Liam, sister Caitlin, and the three boys who live next door.

It's built mostly of cedar, and has lots of windows, even a skylight. He's still working on a secure ladder system. The present ladder is taken into the house at night. *Home Tree Home* was of great assistance in securing the platform, where a combination of fixed and floating methods was utilized.

We have said before how important it is to have healthy host trees, and Alaska has lots of them. In this state species like Sitka spruce, the main source of timber, grow in stands. Its high-grade lumber is prized for its combination of strength and lightness. Before aluminum, it was the main frame material for aircraft.

During a fishing trip to Alaska we met a wonderful character called Gus. Part fisherman and part dog musher, he was staying with our friend John Bramante. Gus had his 18 dogs with him, and in subdivisions around Soldatria neighbors complain about their barking, so his eyes lit up when he heard about the world of treehouse building.

Within a couple of months, Gus had found three spruce-filled acres on the Kenai Peninsula, a mere three hours from Anchorage, and back we came from Seattle to start building his first permanent home. The fun we had building his treehome in the race against the approaching winter is told in *Home Tree Home*.

The Sitkas grew close together, so the plot was chosen by felling some and using them for the supporting beams. The frame was about six feet off the ground, bolted between four trees. Three log posts, embedded on preformed concrete pier blocks, added support.

We had heard that beetlekill blight had been spotted in the area, and avoided the oldest trees since they were the most susceptible to the insects. The trees we used for the foundation still retained their bark, which should have been stripped off before construction as the bark tends to trap moisture. The bark is also a good home to insects and disease, which lead to rot.

The house measured 12-by-16-feet. As each fall night got colder, we worked faster on constructing the frame with lumber that Gus had bartered for some of his spruces. Everything else made its way by pickup truck from Anchorage. Shortly after beginning construction, Gus and his dogs were home, with the spare lumber measured up for him to build doghouses.

Gus had bad luck. As the beetlekill pestilence came closer, he sprayed the trees and had an arborist innoculate them, but the plague was relentless and three of the four supporting trees died. Gus intends to support the house with posts, if and when it becomes necessary. We have learned since that one should first hire an arborist and get the trees checked.

Building the Saltspring treehouse was the central story in *Treehouses*. But apart from a long extension ladder leaning against the trunk, we left it in splendid isolation, so a proper entry was needed after we had put so much effort into the building. The solution was a suspension bridge that started on a slope 60 feet away. Now the treehouse can be approached with dignity and care. Read the sign on the next page.

ONLY TWO PEOPLE ON BRIDGE AT A TIME, FOR SAFETY.

The ladder into the circular treehouse.

One of the two supporting cables running through a guiding block.

The cables are shackled to embedded rock bolts.

up a tree

Up a Tree was an exhibit featuring the work of some San Francisco Bay Area architects. Each design was inspired by one of the regions represented in the Strybing Arboretum & Botanical Garden's diverse plant collections. We were pleased to be invited and a took few pictures.

Koi's Nest
an elliptical treehouse

Here is the statement from Skidmore, Owings and Merrill:

Architecture that is firmly rooted in its place, that organically grows out of its physical setting, is the inspiration for this treehouse design. The Asian influence came from the architect's experiences in Japan, China, and Southeast Asia: the Shinto temples at Ise, the teahouse pavilions on stilts at Katsura, and the tree-dwelling hill tribes in northern Thailand.

The intent of the design is for the treehouse to appear as an organic structure that grows out of its site—a fork in the trunk of a giant eucalyptus tree, 20 feet above the ground. The walls, roof, and floor are latticed redwood boards, allowing every surface to bring in light during the day. In the end, a treehouse is a place to be transformed by the imagination. When the branches are rocking, you might be in a ship at sea. When it's raining and the wind is howling, you might be in the belly of a giant koi, the Japanese fish so powerful it can jump up a waterfall.

Ba House

"Ba" roughly translates from the Japanese as "place."

The following is from the statement by Fernau & Hartman Architects:

. . . This structure is a result of improvisation, with the conjured circumstances of its use, the reality of available materials, and its (temporarily) semi-riparian site. The two main materials, bamboo and milled hardwood, have a "raw" and "cooked" contrast that accentuates the qualities of both. The structural elements are bamboo, connected with cord lashings. The more refined pieces are made from milled mahogany. The only other materials are canvas and a corrugated concrete roof. . . . We have conjured climate as well and taken liberties that evoke much sun, much rain, and a need to capture cooling breezes. The raised vegetal rod structure is nestled into the foliage and sits lightly on the ground—a landed insect on a river of sand.

104

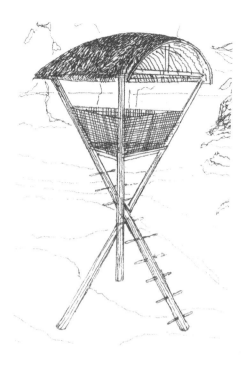

A Simple Hut

This structure was inspired by the Primitive Plant Garden at the arboretum. It has a trapezoid floor at 12 feet, surrounded by rope safety netting, and a palm-frond roof.

G. K. Muennig, the architect, says:
My youth was spent either up a tree or under the ground, spelunking near Joplin, Missouri. From an early age, I had a deep love for nature. While studying with Bruce Goff at the University of Oklahoma, I was inspired to develop a humanistic approach to architecture, in which each structure relates to its natural environment.

The nature of the primitive plant material in the arboretum inspired me to keep my treehouse as natural as possible, from the palm-frond roofing to the poles from fallen trees we collected in a redwood forest. This treehouse is intended to express the beauty of organic architecture.

Domus Eucalyptus

Inspired by Australia

Here is the statement by Richardson Architects:

Two building traditions dominate Australian architecture: the indigenous longhouse and the late 18th- and 19th-century timber-framed house. These two traditions share a number of architectural gestures in response to the tropical environment: stilts to avoid bugs and enhance air movement, open or vented gable ends to release hot air, and louvered wall panels to provide ventilation.

This treehouse design is based on Australian architectural history and the rainbow serpent, a powerful figure in aboriginal myth. This huge snake spent the dry season resting in a deep hole where aborigines feared its wrath should they disturb its slumber. Colored by the rainbow colors of quartz crystals, the immense serpent rose into the sky in the rainy season.

50,000,000 AMERICANS WORK AT HOME in some capacity and it is a growing trend. If you really want to do undisturbed productive work in a place of your own, why not do it up a tree? There might be the occasional interruption from birds tapping on the glass and it is very hard to stop gazing out at the beyond. From our particular experience, the Fall City

Office in a Tree

does work beautifully as an office, and as a showhouse for prospective clients. In this section you will visit some other friends who have made their own writer's aeries, workplaces, and studios off the ground. It's interesting that they all have comfortable beds, too.

Looking for a spot to build our house, we found five acres of pastureland between Seattle and the foothills of the Cascades. On the eastern boundary we were drawn to a stand of large second-growth firs, and even before we broke ground on the house, we built a treehouse office-studio suspended between four of them.

The insulated 15-by-15-foot cabin in the sky is in our favorite shingle style with dark-green trim. Firs standing 125 to 175 feet anchor each corner. It's just 15 feet off the ground.

Just before I get to fit the roof.

A stairway with rope banisters gets you to the front door. Before the office was built, Pete was a purist and would have insisted on a ladder, maybe even a rope ladder. But such ladders are really for kids' treehouses. The stair system has many benefits, especially when you're lifting computer monitors and other equipment up and down—and our dogs like it too. The winding staircase is supported by posts cut from a tree that had to be taken down to make room for the office structure.

During the day we are are often face-to-beak with woodpeckers and wrens on the other side of the glass window. In the evening, after our daughter and twin sons have gone to sleep, the walk across the field creates a change of mood as we go up to the treehouse for some uninterrupted design work at the drafting table, under the glow of green-shaded shop lights.

At break time there's a chance for contemplation on the treehouse's tiny, green-railed porch.

This rendering shows the stairway.

Inside, the office is surprisingly spacious, with enough room for two small desks (one for a custom-built PC and the other outfitted as a drafting table), a file cabinet, a fax machine, a printer, and a reading chair. There is a queen-size bed, which is made up when guests come to stay. Everyone wants to stay here when they visit, and we like to show it off.

Suspended between four trees, the office seems almost big enough to be a weekend home. And on the desk are plans for just such a building—complete with kitchenette, bathroom, fold-down bed, and deck.

John Rouches is our friend and business partner in our ground-based house construction business. But just like us, he likes to work in the trees. With John we built the treehouse office on the side of a hill just below his main house. One side almost rests on terra firma, and the downhill side is 15 feet off the ground.

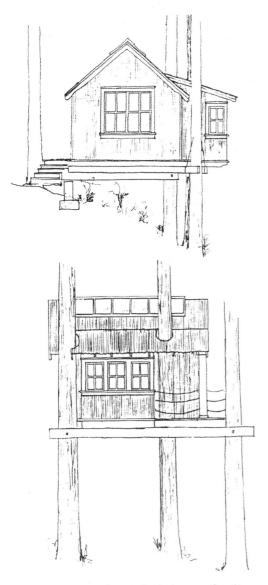

It can be seen that John's love of sailing—
he's a qualified captain—resonates
throughout the interior. Site drawings and
plans are rolled and stowed like navigation
charts, and there's a brass barometer on
the wall. His work area has the feeling of a
captain's cabin in a sailing ship.

Ropes are strung under the rails on the stairway and deck
to complete the nautical look.

At the end of the T-shaped interior, the
double bunk has stowage for bedding.

Out comes the bedding from underneath.

This writer's place of work is in deep seclusion. Imagine a trip by canoe as the first part of the journey, through the woods to a stream; find the *z*-shaped plank bridge, then across a small island, to another wider stream crossed by a narrow, curving, single-planked bridge, and into the woods again to find the treehouse. In deep midwinter snow Stewart Tarry replaces the canoe with cross-country skis. He finds living this far in the New England wilds a necessary ingredient for his literary tasks.

Every plank of the treehouse was carried in his canoe. It helped Stewart to accidently discover the spot as he crossed a pond enlarged by beavers. The building took three years to complete by working in the open seasons, and is now in use throughout the year.

Stewart says that his treehouse is snug at zero degrees or even 10 below. It is a marvel to be gently swayed by the north wind as it rushes through his supporting hemlocks.

The found objects in their place in one room are evidence of Stewart's closeness to nature. Being so far from town, all the books and necessities also become significant and are good to look at. And the beauty outside is far from being a distraction. In fact, his joy of being there best conveyed to us by haiku. Here are five.

sorry, no phone —
out here the chickadees sing
from thin branches

halfway up
four thick hemlocks —
moon in the windows

sunrise dances
across my ceiling —
beavers swimming home

new shadow
across the floor —
first quarter moon

quiet enough
to hear a cat's tongue
behind the woodstove

Adults Keep Out

Children's Treehouses

A wooden treehouse built for kids by themselves, cooperating with other children, or with their grownups is far better than some plastic factory-made article because it becomes a function of their imaginations, as builders and tenants in an imaginary world. Childrens' imaginations take over in the choice or the acquisition of materials. The wood has to be laying around, asked for, or given to them. Memories formed and decisions made in constructing treehouses make kids real builders of society in today's world.

Kid-built in Hawaii.

This is Mackenzie's treehouse. A Long Island artist took three months to build young Mackenzie's den, propped up by an eastern Long Island white oak tree. The eccentrically added trunks and branches cleverly support the structure and add more climbing fun.

There is what looks like a giant birdhouse perched in a backyard tree at the Davis home, in Lansing, Kansas. It officially belongs to Griffin and Gwenna, but it's hard to keep their father down on the ground. Craig Davis had a wistfulness for the treehouse he never had as a child, and the kids knew it.

134

In the week between Christmas and New Year's Day, Griffin said, "Daddy, you told me you'd build me a treehouse when I was six. I'm six and a half and you didn't build it." On New Year's Day, Dad got started. He took inspiration from photos of birdhouses, maybe corncribs and spreads in such magazines as *Country Living*. The goal was to have the tree habitable by the time Griffin turned seven in early April. By devoting every daylight hour between January 1 and April 9 to the treehouse project, Marlene Davis says her husband met his deadline.

Craig's handmade stained-glass window is fitted to the treehouse.

Climbing nets add extra safety to the small deck.

Let's go on a tour of Davis's treehouse, extracted from the visit by Tim Engle of *The Kansas City Star*. First you have to clamber up the big Russian elm a few feet. That's what the attached rope ladder is for. Then, when you get to the fork in the tree, turn around and drop backward into the hammocky cargo net, which doubles as a kid-catcher. Then, according to the treehouse's architect and builder, Craig Davis, it's time to "shimmy up like a crab" through the trapdoor on the house's underside.

If you are over six feet tall you will likely bang your head on the ceiling. When your faculties return, you look around. The 8-by-8-foot interior is carpeted and furnished with a tiny picnic table and two benches. That cute little Elizabethan door that's pointed on top? It leads to the deck, which sticks out about two feet. Two of the walls feature small arched windows that Davis rescued from a church. Another wall glows with a stained-glass bay window. Davis makes these; this one, in fact, was his first.

The door to the deck.

Extra arborial decoration.

The treehouse also has a second floor—more of an attic, really—accessible by ladder. It boasts a skylight. Finally, the house also has a working, if unsophisticated, dumbwaiter of sorts: a wicker basket that can be lowered to the ground with a rope and pulley.

"I wanted to design this thing so it looked kind of whimsical," he says.

"I didn't want it to look like a storage shed in a tree."

140

In appearance it's a "comic-book house," helped along by wavy, scalloped-on-the-bottom siding. It draws children like an ice-cream truck. And a few adults, too. "We've probably had everyone in the neighborhood up there at least once," Marlene says.

The kids do kid things in the treehouse. Griffin and his friends try to keep Gwenna and her friends out. "And the girls try to keep the boys out," Gwenna says.

Gwenna lands safely in the cargo-net kid catcher.

Meanwhile, when the little kids aren't up there, it's likely that a big kid—a 48-year-old kid—will be. Dad finally has a treehouse in his backyard, and it's more spectacular than his grade-school daydreams.

A treehouse at the White House. President Carter and Amy help a little one down.

Our twin sons, Charlie and Henry, gave very important advice, and helped during the construction of their first treehouse.

TOM THUMB HOUSE
1954
Built by Will & Mildred George
For their Thirteen grandchildren
and All other little visitors
in The Forest

We found this tiny house in the trees while hunting for a treehouse in the area, and were taken by the inscription above the door.

The 13 children had wonderful grandparents.

We were travelling through North Carolina when Paul Rocheleau, our photographer friend, saw a sign outside a country house advertising homemade molasses, and his sweet tooth pulled us over. We then saw this kids' clubhouse behind the house next door. The kids' father had found a perfectly good abandoned kindergarten slide and then found a tree for it in his backyard. At the bottom of the slide was a big soft hole full of leaves, indicating many trips down.

An elegantly simple, diamond-shaped treehouse by Joel Seaman rests between a triangle of three cherry trees. The treehouse, built for his son Ethan, has an exterior finished in cedar and a roofline that echoes the main house. But young Ethan had a lot of impact on its finishing touches.

The arrow slits and diamond-shaped windows are made for looking out only. All can be boarded up on the inside. For extra security, the rope ladder is retractable.

What about those strange gutters sloping toward the bucket? Well, Ethan has a two-hole golf course inside, and that's where the putted balls go. When full, the bucket is winched up to the window.

Some adjustment needs to be made on the swinging rope because of the danger of colliding into the treehouse. Joel intends to anchor the rope to the ground to restrict its swing.

Ethan keeps an eye out for intruders from the security of the combined clubhouse and golf course.

154

After sessions on the space trolley and rope, Ethan is ready to settle down with a favorite book.

All over the old logged areas of America, hollow stumps can make great playhouses. At the fine children's summer camp, YMCA Camp Orkila on Orcas Island, Washington, this is where they gather for storytelling on rainy days. A favorite is Shel Silverstein's *The Giving Tree*.

Here, and opposite, you can see the notches made by the lumberjacks' axes to fix supports as they stood and sawed.

A garden treehouse, Bainbridge Island, Washington. The supporting metal brackets were custom-forged.

This is the way up into the treehouse shown on the two preceeding pages. When we got to the top of the ladder, we realized that no adult had ever gotten into it. The last job of the builder was to nail in position the board that kept it as a "kids only" clubhouse.

Safety demands that both adults and children always descend a ladder facing toward the rungs—not looking down like this.

There are occasions when busybodies object to things like this. Here we have a playhouse, or maybe it's an unfinished fort, that was built by youngsters on one of the San Juan Islands, near Seattle. It was accused of being an eyesore by some, but the kids had plenty of local support from other grown-ups, so it still stands as a familiar landmark on the bay. We think that it's a great use of driftwood.

Children love to seek out denlike spaces. By choice they look for old crates, choose to crawl and play under tables, love tents, even try to make their own with an old blanket or sheet. These are special places for themselves and their friends. If they can't get up in a tree, the next best thing is to have

a playhouse on the ground.

They are private, too—no adult can get inside them. When a grown-up tries, it's like a kid trying to get into Snoopy's doghouse. We've built a lot of playhouses, from 5-by-7 feet for preschoolers up to 16-by-16 feet for those with big lawns and lots of kids. They are smaller versions of our treehouse designs and every one follows specifications dictated by our three children. The good news is that playhouses don't need to apply to any code, they are playground equipment.

Three young Nelsons in their den.

How about a playhouse designed by an artist? Barbara Butler dabbled in painting and construction, eventually making colorfully painted custom furniture, which she continues to do. One day she showed up at singer Bobby McFerrin's San Francisco home expecting just to do some renovation work. The singer's wife, Debbie, suggested that she build a playhouse for the couple's two children. That was 10 years ago and the start of a new career. Barbara designs and builds wonderful one-of-a-kind children's play structures all over the country. Her work is noted for its site-specific design, playful proportions, superb craftsmanship, durability, unique harmonies of color, and popularity with kids of all ages. Customers eagerly pay $10,000 to $75,000 for her storybook castles, lighthouses, and elaborate forts, even treehouses! Satisfied clients include Kevin Kline and Phoebe Cates's two children, and a playhouse built by Butler is used in Robin Williams's movie *Bicentennial Man*. Barbara gets grown-ups to behave like big kids. She said to *People* magazine, "When someone says, 'I feel like it's a Matisse in my yard', that's so much better coming from someone who actually owns a Matisse." Debbie McFerrin says Butler's work "looks like it comes from an imaginary indigenous tribe."

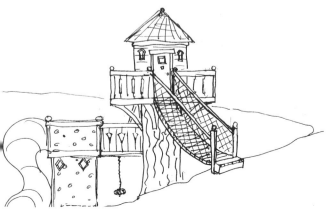

Barbara Butler's sketch for a new playhouse, Canyon Perch, that uses a very large tree stump.

One of Barbara's favorite play-structure features is the ever-popular fire pole.
Each one she installs has a safety gate at the top.

One of Barbara's more ambitious projects, the Hillside Hamlet spans a 40-by-35-foot space nestled into the side of an ivy-covered hill. It has four towers, a crow's nest circling a tree, a two-level hexagonal tower, a rectangular tower, and a landing with stairs leading down to a sandbox area. The unusual black, white, and gray color scheme gives the structure a sort of mystical serenity and complements the colors of the client's home and guest house.

The Hillside Hamlet Crow's Nest is an extension of a bridge leading from the octagonal tower of the Hillside Hamlet, and is mounted completely around the tree trunk. This view of the underside reveals Barbara's artistically beautiful design in combination with her impeccable construction skills.

Seaside Castle.

Malibu Lighthouse.

If the backyard is small, the Robin Hood's Fort fits in a 13'6" x 14'2" space.

The two-story fort includes a who-goes-there peephole, a rock-climbing wall, a bridge over disc swing, 14 cut-out windows, a rope ladder, fire pole, a flagpole with three flags, a secret escape door, a mailbox, and a barred "jail" window.

Right

Since the standard color scheme of Robin Hood's Fort (forest green, ochre, red, and black) seemed too masculine for one second-grade girl, Barbara was delighted to stain it in the girl's favorite colors, pink and purple. Lime, orange, and bright blue accents make this fort particularly vibrant.

The Connecticut Castle.

Barbara designed this play structure not only
to please two boys but also to complement
the beauty of the client's 1910 English-style
stone castle/country home. Tucked in a circle
of trees, the boys' castle has three towers with
a 36-foot slide, a jail with an escape tunnel, a
mad scientist's chamber, four secret doors,
rock-climbing walls, hand-carved gargoyles,
and a 100-foot cable ride from the main
tower into the woods. It's built for the whole
family to play on, kids and adults alike.

Secret Escape Slide (Connecticut Castle).

This secret escape route adds another thrill to
escaping. A foreboding sign (carved with a
slogan specified by the client's two boys) slides
open to reveal the mouth of an escape slide to
the outside.

This is the storybook playhouse. Each of the four walls has a different theme. There is a Dutch door with a working door knocker and a who-goes-there peephole. It's made of redwood throughout. Even the floor is stained a bright color.

Right
The garden playhouse is a simpler version of the storybook playhouse. It is decorated on each side with tulips.

The Rough & Tumble Outpost has three towers, two bridges, two slides, a "jail" with barred windows, a secret door, climbing walls, swinging bridge, crazy climb bars, swings, a fire pole. It's a structure packed with fun features, and built to stand up to the constant play of the five kids who own it and all their friends.

The center tower of the Rough & Tumble Outpost features a clubhouse top and a "jail" with barred windows below. The spiraling ramp, inspired by the Guggenheim Museum, connects the two levels. In back is a turbo tube slide.

The stacking tower of the Rough & Tumble Outpost, shown at right in the original view, has several big steps leading to the top. Each is made with handles and footholds so even the smallest children can climb up.

The Tahoe Tower.
To give kids the fun of
a structure in a small space,
Barbara designed this
hexagonal tower. A long
ramp leads to the top,
where a rope net or a fire
pole allow a route down.
In the back is a turbo tube
slide. The entire tower
features rock-climbing
holds. The bottom of the
tower has all of Barbara's
classic details, including a
mailbox, who-goes-there
peephole in the door, and
cut-out windows.

Rapunzel's Retreat

The Atherton Castle features
two swings, a tube slide, a fire pole,
a stacking fort, a rock-climbing
wall, a flagpole, a bridge over two
swings, shuttered tower windows,
and a two-level fort with open
verandah on top.

Barbara's talent for practical,
appealing design comes through
in every detail. The tower on
the right includes a secret storage
compartment.

Stay in a Treehouse

In a search for the perfect treehouse, one can find a number that are open to the public. These inns—located all over the world—have anywhere from all or few of the comforts of home, along with inspiring views.

The Waipi'o Treehouse Hotel in Hawaii.

The large porch at the Out 'n' About Treesort.

The Out 'n' About Treesort and Treehouse Institute

We first met Michael Garnier in *Treehouses* when Out 'n' About, his unique resort at Takilma, near Cave Junction, Oregon, was doing battle with local building inspectors (referred to as the Tree Stooges), who were unconvinced that his buildings were safe to stay in. It took 66 people, three dogs, a cat, three network TV crews, and the print media—weighing 10,664 pounds—to be part of a stress test up in the uncomplaining Oregon white oak trees. There were many more frustrations and hilarious incidents in the nine-year fight with Josephine County bureaucrats, lawyers, and subpoenaed neighbors, but today, for the moment, all is well as the county has ruled that the buildings of Out 'n' About are safe and sound.

Out 'n' About has expanded its activities. It was always an adventurous vacation spot, and today it is also the headquarters of the Out 'n' About Treehouse Institute of Takilma. Michael's pioneering work on behalf of treehouses brings us together as founding members of the World Treehouse Association Annual Conference, where we lecture on and participate in treehouse building and tree care, all the while learning from each other. The Treehouse Institute invites treehouse lovers and guests to participate in courses on treeminology, forest ecology, performing arts, crafts, equestrianism, physical education, home economics, and we're sure, there'll be more. All guests are invested as Tree Musketeers. You will have a wonderful time, and watch out for the puns on the word "tree"—they come thick and fast.

A treeology class in action.

Here is Michael Garnier's description of Out 'n' About.
There are many educational, and adventurous, vacation
sites in Southern Oregon, but only one where you can,
lit-treely "go out on a limb"—and learn something while
you're there.

The internationally famous Out 'n' About Treesort has
branched out once again, and is now Out 'n' About
Treehouse Institute of Takilma, a high school that hangs
from the branches in an oak grove in Takilma, a
picturesque little valley nestled among the Siskiyou
Mountains, just below the headwaters of the east fork of
the Illinois River.

The Institute features Treehouse Dormitrees to
accommodate student families. There are also two units
for nonstudents, though students may stay in them as
well. The Tree Room Schoolhouse Suite (which includes
a bathroom, kitchenette, and "sitting-to-ponder area"),
the Swiss Family Complex (a pair of treehouses connected by a swinging bridge), and the "Treepee" are for
treesidential students only and require a minimum two-
day stay. (Summer thematic school sessions, in majors and
alltreenut majors, run from two to four days.) Also
available are the Peacock Perch (designed for, and best
enjoyed by, two—very romantic) and the Cabintree
(a deluxe "on-the-ground" gem accompanied by an
open-air treehouse).

The Treehouse Institute, established over the summer of 1996, offers avocational instruction in basic engineering, design, and construction methods for building treehouses (Treeology I), and teaches some of the tricks to getting treehouses approved by building departments (Treeology II), and root words (Treeminology).

There is also a library, with books about treehouses and a section that traces the histree, both physical and political, of Out 'n' About.

In the Swiss Family Complex, the children's unit has an undersized door and built-in bunk beds. The adult unit is entered via a trapdoor in the floor and has a deck that is accessed through a French door. A combination deck/landing below the adults' unit supports the swinging bridge to the kids' room. From a second, lower, landing, children of all ages can swoop to the yard area on a rope swing.

194

The Peacock Perch has a double bed, hand-washing sink, and small porch/landing at the top of the 20-foot-high pole-banistered stairs. It is touched off nicely by a hand-carved door highlighted by a giant peacock.

An engineering marvel, the
Tree Room Schoolhouse
Suite has its own bathroom,
complete with antique claw-foot
cast-iron tub, a kitchenette that
includes refrigerator, microwave,
coffeemaker, and toaster (bring
your own utensils and plates),
separate master bedroom, a
double futon in the sitting area,
and a loft that accommodates
two children.

The interior and steps of the Tree Room Schoolhouse.

The "Treepee" is 9 feet in diameter, 8 feet off the ground, and sleeps two to four children. It has a deck out the canvas door and is entered via a ladder, through a flap at floor level. The tepee is 18 feet in diameter and sleeps four easily. It has a bed, fire pit, and electricity. This unit is available summer months only.

All students at the Treehouse Institute of Takilma have complete run of the facility through the physical-education department. There are barbecues, picnic tables, a dirt basketball court, and a unique, stone-lined, chemical-free swimming pool that is fed by the nearby Illinois River.

The two-story Cabintree, which sleeps five comfortably, faces away from the rest of the facility and commands a view of a large meadow and an old-growth-covered mountainside. It also serves as the study hall. A "cabintreehouse" is perched to its side and is treeserved for young cabin dwellers—adults by invitation only. The cabin is log-framed, has a kitchenette and bathroom, and is touched off by striking rockwork behind the Franklin Fireplace.

A "cabintreehouse" near the Cabintree.

In Hawaii, the tiny ## Waipi'o Treehouse Hotel
on the Big Island is truly unique in that one of its rooms is 30 feet above ground in a monkeypod tree. Inside, the house has the feel of a cabin cruiser, complete with running water, small kitchen, VCR, and a very comfortable queen-size bed. There is a separate Japanese-style bathhouse replete with soaking tubs and thick towels. This is shared with the second, ground-based room called the Hali, which is beautiful unto itself. If the treehouse is booked, the Hali makes a wonderful backup. The house faces a thousand-foot waterfall called Papala, Hawaiian for "radiant." Pools at the bottom provide swimming and drinking water.

The dream of escape is certainly part of the attraction of Waipi'o Treehouse. The operative word is "transformation," says Linda Beech, owner of the hotel. "There are some very lyrical things that have been said about it. An oncologist and a first violin came to stay with us. They were married, and this is what they left in the guest book: 'A physician came here and was healed; a musician came here and heard the music.' "

"I'm a doctor of psychology. We have from our possibly arboreal ancestors, certainly from our DNA, this kind of physiological need to be in totally pure surroundings. Our concept of Eden is so archetypal around the world that some-how it must be something we need."

The hotel is far enough off the beaten track that a four-wheel-drive vehicle must bring guests into the valley, one of the first to be occupied when Polynesians came to Hawaii, and now home to much of the islands' archeological history.

As is true with any treehouse, occupants in the Waipi'o Hotel are closer to nature and sometimes have to accommodate themselves to the natural world. The hotel warns its guests that "occasionally, a few days a year, Waipi'o Treehouse is inaccessible because of high river water. Should guests be unable to leave, food and lodging during their delay are complimentary.

The Tarzan House at the

Ariau Jungle Lodge in Amazonas sits a serene 100 feet above ground in the middle of the Brazilian jungle. Mounted without cutting or perforating its supporting tree, the treehouse offers water, electric lighting, a ceiling fan and total security to its guests. The Tarzan House is perhaps more modern, but not unlike the lofty structures built by men harvesting rubber to protect themselves from the jungle's predatory animals during the rubber boom in the Amazon.

From the treehouse's perch is a bird's-eye view of the Amazon jungle, the Rio Negro and Parana Rivers, the Furo River that connects them, as well as the Ariau River. Six friendly species of monkey, some macaws, and coatimundis make their home at the nearby lodge.

The treehouses of **Hotel Hana Iti** are built in banyan trees and giant acacias. Romantic and comfortable, this Tahitian sanctuary of solitude conforms to the shapes and spaces of the trees around it, and with largely open walls, maximizes the view across the sea to the neighboring island. Natural wood furnishings covered in fine fabrics complement high, airy, thatch roofs.

The setting for Hana Iti couldn't be more ideal with Tahiti's diverse landscape of sea-level coral atolls, volcanic mountain peaks, white-sand beaches, brilliant turquoise lagoons, lush green hills, and abundant flowering plants. The height of buildings on the islands is restricted to the height of the tallest palm tree, providing optimal conditions to view French Polynesia's breathtaking environment.

The six tree huts that sit 50 feet above ground in Thailand's **Khao Sok National Park** offer a full view—through their unique walls that open up and out—of the jungle canopy. Accessed by ladder, the Treehouse Lodge's sleeping quarters are comfortable and simply built, with sleeping room for two in each hut, thatch roofs, Asian-style bathrooms, and no electricity.

A veritable Yosemite of the jungle, Khao Sok's dramatic karst limestone cliffs, tranquil pools, caves, waterfalls, and wildlife set in virgin rain forest make inevitable a peaceful escape from the modern world. Seasoned guides aid adventurers in exploring the surrounding national treasure.

Right: The Cedar Creek Treehouse.

The Japanese believe that magnificent views should not come easily—one should work to attain them. That is precisely what Bill Compher achieved when, after much travail, he could at last stand, halfway up a 100-foot cedar, on one of the braces that would support the floor of his treehouse and take in views of Mount Rainier in the distance.

The Cedar Creek Treehouse

is 16-by-16 feet, features a living room, bathroom, kitchen, and an attached sunroom/viewing room which often serves as a makeshift bedroom. On the main floor, food is kept cool in an icebox and cooked on a four-ring butane stove. A second-story loft, outfitted with sleeping necessities, easily accommodates four more people. Solar panels power 12-volt electric lights. The water container is raised by rope and pulley. Compher's highly detailed and thoroughly impressive work is not quite in keeping with the "bare necessities" formula of the average treehouse master plan. For it is in fact one of the most charming getaways in America, on or above land. A quick read of the guest book—comments from honeymooners, families young and old, and trekkers from nearby Mount Rainier National Park—tells of the joy of staying in this hideaway in the sky.

Originally, reaching the treehouse required a vertical climb up steps attached to the tree trunk, and then through a trapdoor. When his mother-in-law froze on the steps about 30 feet up, the builder realized that his future plans for the guest house would be compromised unless he lessened the burden of ascension. His solution: a stairway with landings offering panoramic views, a glassed-in observation deck adorned with chairs and a hammock, and a catwalk leading to the front door.

Looking out from the living room toward the catwalk that connects the climbing tower.

A view of the main floor showing the stairway to the sleeping loft. The massive cedar tree is always a presence, growing through the floor and out the roof. A benefit from the growing trunk is the tight fit of the surrounding carpet. Climbing field mice looking for crumbs can no longer squeeze through the gap.

Constructing this treehouse was an enormous undertaking, and Compher fully deserves the praise and attention it has received from the Pacific Northwest media and *Fine Homebuilding* magazine. In particular, they were impressed that he was able to hoist up the lumber with a single pulley, one piece at a time—a Sisyphean process he doesn't recommend.

The starlit and carpeted sleeping loft with a reading lamp for cloudy nights.

Another wonderful feature is its glassed-in sleeping porch, complete with breathtaking views of the creek below.

One way up and one way down—the catwalk connecting the observation deck to the stairway.

Treehouse builders often have interesting stories to tell about their experiences in the woods, and Compher's troubling tale, which began just after the treehouse was completed, is surely one of the most engaging. One afternoon, an army helicopter flew over, then another, lower and noisier, then more, always hovering and completely shattering the peace in their retreat. Initially, given that the structure is in clear view of the pilots that regularly fly in and out of nearby Fort Lewis on training flights, Compher accepted the pilots' curiosity. But he also knew that these pilots were straying from their flight path by a few miles. Eventually, the earsplitting noise got to Compher. "I called the Pentagon collect," he said. "The operator told me that she could not accept collect calls. I said I was being attacked." This tactic worked and he actually got to speak to someone who promised to investigate the complaint. Still, weeks later, rotors roared above Compher's treehouse. Outraged, he contacted his congressman, invited representatives from the Army, and local radio and television reporters to meet at the treehouse to try to put an end to the aerial harassment. Finally, the Comphers won back their peace and tranquility.

Building houses on the West Coast and putting up treehouses all over the world takes a lot of coordinating. Under the platform on the left is our partner in the treehouse building company Treehouse Workshop LLC, Jake Jacob. He is always out ahead of us, meeting customers, checking sites, and doing all the organizing.

Resources:
American Arborists Supplies, Inc.
 1-800-441-8381
Treehouse Workshop LLC
 Jake Jacob and Pete Nelson
 www.treehouseworkshop.com
Michael Garnier
 www.treehouses.com
 1-800-200-5484

Please send interesting photos to:
 Peter and Judy Nelson
 P.O. Box 1136
 Fall City, WA 98024

Since *Treehouses* and *Home Tree Home,* our work out on a limb has blossomed into putting up many more treehouses. At the World Treehouse Association, we are constantly hearing about more. This book shows many examples from our new friends in the treehouse world. In alphabetical order, we would like to thank the following for their help, encouragement, letters, journals, and pictures:

Ralph Armstrong
Alan Beal
Linda Beech
Joy Bennett
Darryl Boyd
Paul E. Brozen
Linda Butler
Barbara Butler
Dale and Sue Carrington
Suki Casanave
Clark Casebolt
Jim Casebolt
Debra Cash
The Jimmy Carter Museum
Mike Caveney
Bill Compher
Carl Cook
Craig Davis
David DeBella
Don Duncan
Eco Traveller
Tim Engle
Hollis L. Engley
Fine Homebuilding
Patrick Fulton
Michael Garnier
Randy Geiger
Katsuhiko Harada
Ian Jones
The Kansas City Star

The Kellogg Family
Thomas Kern
John Kirchmier III
Takashi Kobayashi
Sun LaMaster
M.L. Lyke
John MacKenzie
Spike Mafford
Ed McBee
Norm Nelson
Tom Ness
Matt Peters
Steve Rice
Nat Ross
John Rouches
Matt and Gretchen Scoble
The Scurlock Family
Joel Seaman
Chris Skotheim
Tom and Sue Smith
Mark Terry
Tour India
Mark Trumbell
The Wall Street Journal
Logan Ward
The Ware Family
The Wyckoff Family

GLOSSARY

Adze: a hatchetlike tool used to flatten wood surfaces.

Arborist: a tree-care expert and invaluable resource.

Arresting chain: a safety mechanism used in conjunction with the floating-point load foundation system.

Barge boards: the finishing boards that attach to the ends of a gabled roof.

Barge rafter: the outermost rafter of a gabled roof.

Beam: a horizontal structural element in construction upon which rest floor or deck joists, or roof rafters. Beams are supported by walls or posts.

Blocking: framing elements often used between studs and floor joists to help strengthen walls and floors, and to slow fires from rising.

Bottom plate: the framing member that runs the length of a wall at its base.

Bowline knot: a simple knot that can take a lot of weight or stress but unties easily.

Carabiner: a metal loop, typically used by rock climbers, that opens and closes to hold lines.

Ceiling joist: the horizontal framing member that rests on the top plate of a wall and spans from one wall to another.

Climber's knot: a self-hoisting friction knot commonly used by arborists.

Come-along: a winchlike tool used to move or lift heavy objects.

Common studs: the vertical framing members used in an ordinary wall layout.

Door casing: the trim material that wraps around the sides and top of a door.

Draw knife: a straight blade about 12 to 16 inches in width with a handle on each end. Used to take bark off trees.

Fixed-point load: a rigid bolt connection between a wooden beam and a tree.

Flashing: strips of thin metal usually applied under roofing and siding to repel water from walls and windows.

Floating-point load: a connection between a beam and a tree that allows a certain amount of movement for both the beam and the tree to which it is connected.

Floor joist: a structural framing member that typically runs on edge and supports the floor. Joists in turn are supported by beams or walls.

Flush: even with one another.

Gable: the pointed end of a building that is created by the meeting of two roof planes.

Hauling lines: lines used to lift material and tools to a desired location.

Header: the framing member placed above doors and windows that is used to support the extra downward forces created by a break in the standard spacing of the studs.

Hip rafter: the roof rafter created where two roof planes come together, and where that is not considered a peak or a ridge.

Jamb: the vertical frame of a door or a window.

King stud: a framing member used in conjunction with a jack stud to support a window or door header.

Knee brace: a support post that angles back from and below the beam it supports to the trunk of the tree.

Lag bolt: a large screw with a square head.

Lanyard: a safety rope used when securing oneself above the ground.

On edge: position of a piece of lumber when it supports weight on its narrow side.

Outriggers: the framing members that span outside the exterior wall line to support a building's eave and barge rafter.

Pitch: the slope of a roof.

Plumb: level in the vertical plane.

Plumb line: a tool that has a teardrop-shaped weight at the end of a string; used to find the level on the vertical plane.

Posting down: using a post to support a horizontal span of a beam.

Ridge cap: the uppermost part of roofing that covers the roof ridge.

Rim joist: joist that caps the ends of the common joists on both sides.

Roof trusses: prefabricated roof supports that sit on the top plate of a wall or on a beam.

Scribing: process of marking and cutting wood to accommodate an irregularly shaped intrusion, such as the trunk of the tree or its branches.

Sheathing: the wood, typically plywood, used as an underlayment to siding or roofing. It is applied directly to the frame of the structure.

Shim: a thin, wedge-shaped piece of wood, typically cedar, used in a door or window jamb to create a flat and nailable spacer.

Sill: a horizontal framing member at the base of a window's rough framing.

Skip sheathing: a method of roofing or siding that uses alternating rows of sheathing and open spaces.

Sliding slot: a method of attaching a beam to a tree in which the main bolt(s) slides in a horizontal slot, giving the beam and tree some flexibility.

Spacers: short sections of galvanized pipe that thread over bolts and hold beams away from trees so trees have room to grow.

Speed square: an essential carpentry tool that allows quick 90- and 45-degree markings on framing lumber.

Stringers: the sides of a stair upon which the treads and risers rest.

Suspended-point load: a method of attachment where the beams are suspended by cables.

Top plate: the framing member that runs the length of the wall along the top.

Tree-grip dead end: a preformed cable splicer that creates a strong loop at the end of the cable.

Umbrella foundation: a style of framework used in building in one tree without posting down to ground. The beams together form an umbrella pattern, with the tree at the center.

Wainscoting: the lower segment of an interior wall that differs from the rest of the wall.

Wind shear: the force on a building created by wind.

Window casing: the trim used around the interior and exterior of a window.

*There's a yearning for treehouses out on the prairie.
If you can't find a tree, you can always build one.*

PHOTO CREDITS